The Valued Self

The Valued Self

Five Steps to Healthy Self-Esteem

Value Processing Therapy© (VPT)

Includes The Valued Self Workbook ©

Dr. Elliott B. Rosenbaum

iUniverse, Inc.
Bloomington

The Valued Self
Five Steps to Healthy Self-Esteem

iUniverse books may be ordered through booksellers or by contacting:

iUniverse
1663 Liberty Drive
Bloomington, IN 47403
www.iuniverse.com
1-800-Authors (1-800-288-4677)

ISBN: 978-1-4620-3697-4 (sc)
ISBN: 978-1-4620-3698-1 (ebk)

Printed in the United States of America

iUniverse rev. date: 08/04/2011

Contents

PART III–The Valued Self© Appendices

“I get out my work and have a show for myself before I have it publicly. I make up my own mind about it—how good or bad or indifferent it is. After that, the critics can write what they please. I have already settled it for myself so flattery and criticism go down the same drain and I am quite free!”

Georgia O’Keeffe
1887-1986

Introduction

As a younger man, my personal self-growth process led me to devote myself to the traditional training of a psychologist. I began working with patients as a graduate student and wondered if the self-esteem issues that plagued me as a teenager and young adult were common. I wondered how I could help my patients through the same processes that had helped me. I wanted to help others achieve happiness in their lives, and my research led me to the following clue: I found that my clients were almost all suffering from low self-esteem.

When they evaluated themselves, they came up short and found themselves lacking in many different ways.

I found that the standards these clients used to measure themselves were more the problem than anything else. I came to believe that most of us are completely unaware of the many standards by which we appraise ourselves. We measure ourselves by our looks, our popularity, our money, status and job. Most of all, we measure ourselves based on how we perceive others judge us. This leaves us in a constant state of anxiety, wondering where we will fall short next. Most of us are under the control of these many self-measurements (and self-criticisms) and we often feel that there is little room for us to be ourselves.

What further complicates this is the fact that most of us have no idea that we are enslaved to these many masters. As a therapist, my first objective is to help my clients become aware of their constant self-measurements ("Am I rich enough, smart enough, good-looking enough, likeable enough, etc.?"). A secondary objective is to provide my clients with a clear look at how their self-measurement criteria often make it impossible for them to feel good about themselves.

This book, and the process it describes, is designed to be a solution to this common problem. It aims at helping you find a life mission that will serve as your primary self-measurement criteria. This mission is a self-chosen standard to live by that is a true reflection of your personal values and goals. Having a life mission to guide our lives allows us the freedom from external measurements, especially other people's judgments.

When a person has a clear and inspiring life mission, and uses this as their primary self-measurement criteria, disapproval from others does not hold the same power over them. Through this work, external judgments begin to feel irrelevant to one's values, mission and goals. *The result of this work is emotional freedom—a sense of clear life direction and an overall, stable sense of wellbeing and self-worth, which I refer to as the Valued Self.*

This short book is an introduction to a method of talk therapy that I have developed over the years. This method is an existential-humanistic method that is most closely related to Viktor Frankl's "Logotherapy." I refer to this method as Value Processing Therapy (VPT) because the goal of this therapy is to identify, evaluate and modify the system which each of us utilizes to give ourselves value. This therapy has also been applied to multiple settings including organizational settings as well as to life coaching. In these settings, I refer to this method as the Valued Self Method, which this book outlines.

The first part of the book provides thirty points on the Valued Self map. Each point is designed to be read and processed by the reader in a way that will serve as the knowledge base for properly making the best use of Part II of the book, the Valued Self Workbook. The Valued Self Workbook can be filled out individually, though for maximum benefit, I highly recommend completing it with a therapist or coach who is trained in the Valued Self Method. Interested parties may contact the author regarding research conducted on Value Processing Therapy (VPT) as this is an ongoing project.

Acknowledgments

I thank G-d and my parents, Magda and Jerry Rosenbaum, for everything they have done to get me to this point.

A special thank you to my editors (MR, ER, and NK), my teachers, my students and my clients.

I dedicate this book to my soul-mate, Emily, and to my wonderful children.

PART I

The Valued Self©

1

My Journey

> "It's not who you are that holds you back, it's who you think you're not." ~Author Unknown

Let me share with you a snapshot of a trend that I noticed in my life a number of years ago. It may seem somewhat familiar to you.

When I was in eight grade, the key to popularity was basketball. The kids who were good at basketball were "cool." I really wanted to be cool, but alas, since I was not good at basketball—I was not cool. When I was in tenth grade, being popular with girls was the way to achieve popularity. Since I was popular with girls, I was "cool" and as a result of this, my self-esteem soared. After high school, a high level of value was placed on being accepted to an "Ivy League" university by friends and family. I was not a very conscientious student at the time, and was lucky to be accepted to a non-Ivy League school. As a result, I did not feel very good about myself. After college, status appeared to come from how much money one made, and since I was broke, my self-esteem suffered.

I could give many examples of experiences throughout my life that impressed on me some specific standard with which I was supposed to measure my self-worth. I know now that this process caused me endless anguish, as my self-esteem seemed to shift drastically from environment to environment.

These experiences impressed on me many <u>standards</u> with which I was supposed to measure my self-worth.

By the time I reached my early twenties, I was emotionally exhausted. I was finding it impossible to satisfy the expectations of all of the different people and environments which had something to say about what makes me valuable—status, looks, money, power, education, you name it. I was trapped and depressed by this prison of impossible expectations and I did not even know it.

My escape came around this time when a friend recommended a therapist who specialized in early adulthood issues. This therapist listened intently to my life story and then asked me to do something that changed my life: he asked me to go home and think about what my life purpose was, and to write it down as a Mission Statement.

After much thought, I wrote on a piece of paper that my mission in life is "to use my talents to help others come closer to their life purpose."

This defining moment brought into focus the fact that I had been a slave to the many masters of others' expectations and that I had allowed these expectations to bully me into submission. As I began to fashion my life around this newfound purpose, I was able to slowly stop carrying the expectations that my environment sought to impose on me, especially those that were not relevant to my life purpose. This freedom brought with it an emotional stability and confidence which I had never known before and which has defined my life ever since.

I offer you this book as a guide to help you clarify your own life purpose. Your life purpose will guide you as you develop goals for every sphere of your life. You will then learn to measure your self-worth using standards that match your deepest values. The result will invariably be a wonderful gift to yourself and to those you love—your Valued Self.

The next chapter will give you a broad overview of the Valued Self Method, which you will be exposed to again in the second part of this book, the Valued Self Workbook.

2

Overview—The Valued Self Method in Five Steps

- Step 1—*Identify Your Self Evaluation System*. Here you will take an honest accounting of all the different criteria that you use to measure your self-worth. They will likely be a combination of your true values, or Core Values, and values that you perceive others (including society) expect from you or value you for, or External Values.
- Step 2—*Identify your Core Values*. You will differentiate between your External Values and Core Values in your Self Evaluation System. You will also add additional ideal Core Values to your Core Values System that are not yet part of your Self Evaluation System.
- Step 3—*The Mission Statement*. You will craft your Core Values into a Mission Statement that encompasses these Core Values. This will be an aspirational statement that describes what you want to accomplish with your life. It will guide your decisions depending on whether the choice in front of you adds or detracts from your life mission. Through repeatedly using this mission as the standard by which you measure yourself by, you will develop your Valued Self. External Values and judgments will begin to hold little to no power over you as you integrate this mission into your thinking and allow it to become your primary guide in life.
- Step 4—*Goal Setting*. The next step is to explore real ways to express and fulfill your mission in your life. This means making

a list of concrete goals in all areas of your life that will fulfill your values and life mission.

- Step 5—*Identifying and Removing Blocks*. The final step is to discover the reasons and life factors that are getting in the way of fulfilling this mission and expressing it in life through your goals. These blocks can be environmental (poor social support, negative relationships, finances) or psychological (negative self-talk, harsh self-criticism, projections from your past). Negative self-talk is worked on in this stage to make our self-statements more in line with our life mission. Many people have found working with a therapist or life coach most helpful for this stage.

3

Jennifer's Story

Jennifer has been a client of mine for ten months. She is a successful business executive in her forties, has two children, and has been married for twelve years. She came to me for help with her marriage. She felt that her poor relationship with her husband was making her more and more anxious and she was starting to display some obsessive-compulsive behavior such as cleaning her house compulsively.

During my initial assessment, Jennifer reported that her parents had taught her to be a "good girl" and that this required her to always put other peoples' needs above hers. She admitted that this was the case with her husband, and that she felt that she had given up her dreams in favor of his. When I asked her about her dreams, Jennifer told me that she never really thought about this and was not really sure what she wanted. She had always relied on her environment to tell her what was valuable and therefore had never taken the time to listen to what fulfilled her. She also reported that she had chronic low self-esteem because she never could measure up to being a "good girl" which was actually a way of saying "pleasing everybody all the time."

We made a plan to work on her Core Values, Mission Statement and goals in addition to marital therapy. I explained to her that the main ingredient to having successful relationships is a sense that we are valued in our relationships. I also explained that in order to feel valued by others, we must be able to value ourselves, otherwise, we will not be able to accept the positive feedback we receive from others. Jennifer worked on developing her Core Values, crafted a Mission Statement and identified her goals. She also identified the External Values that would be the source of negative self-criticism ("being a good girl") and began working through these criticisms with me using Cognitive-Behavioral Therapy. She also began communicating her needs and goals to her husband during this process.

After ten months, Jennifer's anxious and obsessive behavior has almost completely stopped. She reports having a better relationship with her husband and a strong sense of self-worth. While Jennifer is still working on feeling comfortable with not pleasing others' expectations all the time, she now sees this as an External Value. She recognizes that this External Value does not have to be satisfied since it is not compatible with her life mission of "Using my gifts to help women achieve financial and emotional independence, while caring for my spiritual, emotional and physical well-being."

4

Identifying Your Values

As children, we were like sponges, constantly absorbing information from our environment. When our parents smiled at certain actions, we learned that these actions were value enhancing, and when our parents frowned, we learned to stop doing whatever we were doing. We received similar messages from siblings, peers, teachers and the media. We learned what was appropriate, what was acceptable and what was desirable. We also experienced good feelings from engaging in certain actions and this information was also stored away in our minds. As we matured, the rules for what was desirable and what was not, became etched in our minds as an intricate system of Do's and Don'ts. Most adults, in fact, continue to live by these rules, exactly as they were laid down for them as children. Sometimes, these rules are a good fit for their core personalities, although often they are not.

> *Jacob, a 28 year-old man with a degree in accounting, was still living at home with his parents. He had not started working as an accountant and when he came to see me, told me that he dreads the thought of working as an accountant. When I asked him why he chose accounting, he said he was unsure, but remembered that his father always spoke highly of their family accountant. When probed about his Core Values, Jacob identified "creativity." He also reported*

> *that when he would excitedly come home with artwork as an adolescent, though his parents were always polite, he often felt that he was disappointing them by focusing on art and not on "more practical subjects." Through our work together, Jacob realized that he had denied his Core Value of creativity because he felt that others did not value it. When he began looking at other important values, he realized that there were many aspects of his personality, interests and values that were not being realized.*

The first step in the development of the Valued Self is taking a hard look at the reality of your self-definition and specifically, the criteria by which you consciously and subconsciously measure yourself. This requires you to gain access to the complicated self-evaluation system that your psyche employs. For example, many young women today measure their self-esteem by their physical attractiveness. They have, usually subconsciously, assessed that society values them by this standard and, again subconsciously, have accepted this standard as their own. Women, who then perceive themselves to be unattractive, feel a low sense of worth.

The insight here is that the value that they are using is "attractiveness." What I am asking you to do is to take an accounting of all the different standards that you use to value yourself. People who do this honestly, often find that they have been subservient to too many masters. That is, they have had to satisfy too many conditions, and too many people, in order to feel good about themselves. Board game creators discovered long ago, that the best selling games are neither too hard nor too easy. Are the rules which govern your self-esteem set up in a way that make it impossible for you to score any points with yourself? In my experience as a psychologist, I have found that this is often the cause of depression and anxiety for many of my clients. They are depressed that they have not scored any self-esteem points with themselves, and are anxious that they will fail in this respect again in the future. The problem here is not the player, the problem is that the rules are too hard, if not impossible.

We had to satisfy too many conditions, and too many people, in order to feel good about ourselves.

5

Core Values vs. External Values

As children, we constantly looked to others to tell us what was expected of us. On a deeper level, what we were asking was "what do I have to do for you to value me?" We carefully collected all of the information we received as an answer to this question. We then used this information to create a set of standards to serve as the basis for how we measure our value. As children, we did not have the tools to critically evaluate these standards and ask ourselves if these standards were in our best interest or not. As adults, we are able to question these standards and decide if these standards are consistent with our values and goals. As adults, we recognize that we can no longer rely on others and our environment to tell us how to value ourselves. The consequences of doing so are far too serious and include living a life that we feel disconnected from, as well as a sense that we are living someone else's life and are giving up on being ourselves in the deepest sense.

In order to regain control of our Value, we must analyze the value system that we employ and against which we measure ourselves. Most of us find that there are two general categories of values that make up our Self Evaluation System (SES). First, there are values that we feel truly connected with. When we act according to these values we feel we are connecting to our life purpose. We notice ourselves acting according to these values because we really believe in them, not because somebody is watching us and not for some type of reward. I call these your Core Values.

In order to regain control of our Value, we must analyze the value system against which we measure ourselves.

At the same time, we all have values that have been taught to us by others or by society which do not feel connected to our Core. We feel compelled to satisfy these standards, but only because satisfying them brings some form of external reward or avoids an external punishment. For instance, picture a person who grows up to believe they are a complete failure if something they do is not done perfectly. This person will likely develop perfectionism as a value. Since he does not feel connected to this value and because it is self-criticism that drives him to satisfy this value, we would consider his perfectionism an External Value. This value generally hurts his self-esteem, and he feels resentful towards it. The definition of an External Value, therefore, is a value that is either in conflict or which is irrelevant to one's Core Values.

6

The Self-Esteem Meter

One of the biggest problems with allowing others' judgments to serve as the basis for our self-worth is the negative impact this has on our self-esteem. Self-esteem has long been recognized as the foundation for mental health. Richard Gardner, a prominent child psychologist, wrote that all of the disorders he treated in children over the span of four decades were rooted in poor self-esteem. When the self-esteem improved, the negative symptoms went away. People who feel good about themselves are successful, healthy and fun to be with and therefore attract good things into their lives. The opposite is true of people with poor self-esteem, they report more depression, anxiety, health problems and unstable relationships.

I find the concept of a self-esteem meter to be helpful and I ask my clients how full their self-esteem meter is. I also ask them what fills their meter up and what makes it go down. Clients who judge themselves based on other peoples' opinions often find that their self-esteem meter appears to have a leak, and that it is virtually impossible for them to feel good about themselves. It is too hard to please everybody, especially since people often want you to do things that go against what you know to be your true life purpose. This is one the primary reasons why developing a clear Mission Statement is so important.

It is too hard to please everybody, especially since others often want you to do things that go against what you know to be your true life purpose.

This mission should serve as the primary measure of your self-esteem. When you are fulfilling your mission, your self-esteem meter should go up, when you are not, it should go down and remind you to get back to your life mission. Someone who has a clear life mission and has integrated this into their psyche as their sole self-measurement standard will have full control over their self-esteem. Other people's opinions will not matter, since most people know that their life purpose is not "to please everybody."

7

Developing a Mission Statement

The ideal Mission Statement encompasses all that you truly value: your spiritual, emotional, physical and relational goals are all included in this grand mission. Having identified your Core Values will make crafting a Mission Statement much easier. The goal here is to distill the essence of all the Core Values and goals you have into one or two sentences that say it all. These sentences should be phrased positively, for example: "to be a great husband" as opposed to "to not upset my wife." Mission Statements that are inspirational tend to be the most effective kind.

The Mission Statement should be simple enough that you can commit it to memory. It should be easy to recall, especially when you feel confused or become aware that you are judging yourself according to old self-measurements (External Values). Your Mission Statement is the new measuring stick against which you will measure yourself and which your self-esteem should be based on. Some people have a tendency to beat themselves up for not having fulfilled their Mission Statement yet, and for this reason it is crucial that your statement imply that you will engage *in the process* and not be focused on achieving the goal. While the effort is in your control, the results are not. Since you will be basing your self-esteem on this, it is imperative that you have control over the actions required to fill your self-esteem meter up.

John is a 36-year-old sales representative with very poor self-esteem. He chronically beats himself up over not being in a serious relationship. He desperately wants to be married and have children but finds that his poor self-confidence makes it almost impossible for him to meet women. When I asked him to develop a mission statement, he wrote: "to be a kind and loving person and to be a great husband and father". I helped John realize that while being a great husband and father were important Core Values, since he is not in a relationship, his mission statement would likely make him feel worse. John revised his mission statement to "to always strive to be a kind and loving person in the service of others."

8

Run Your Life Like a Business

Many businesses have adopted a Mission Statement. This statement summarizes everything that the business wishes to accomplish. It does not spell out the details of how this will get accomplished, it only gives an aspirational picture of what the company is all about. Any employee who loses his way and becomes confused with what he is supposed to be doing can just look at the Mission Statement and he will be instantaneously placed back on track.

Most of us agree that this is a good way to run a business, but when it comes to running our own lives, we flounder around for purpose and direction. We receive multiple pieces of mixed messages from various sources and try to cram all of that into a confused and unconscious source of direction. Of course we would never run a business like this unless we wanted to go bankrupt, but we feel quite comfortable doing this with our lives. Having a clear life mission makes it easier to stay on track: all major and minor decisions are weighed against this mission. If it furthers the mission, then the path is chosen, if not, then this path is rejected.

Having a clear life mission makes it easier to stay on track: all major and minor decisions are weighed against this mission.

9

The 85-Year-Old Test

Picture yourself being 85 years old, sitting on a rocking chair while reviewing your life. What are the things that you will wish you had accomplished? What will give you a sense of having lived your life with meaning and purpose? If you view your life as a journey with a final destination, what is that destination? Most people have not clarified these questions in their minds, and as a result, they find themselves drifting through life, starting and stopping projects seemingly on a whim. The antidote to this is the clarity we are talking about in this book.

Think about how much easier making decisions would be if you had a clear life mission. You could ask yourself in those moments of indecision, does this choice take me a step closer to my ultimate goal, or does it take me a step further away? Imagine how few moments of self-doubt you would have and how strong you would be even when facing opposition.

Most people have not clarified these questions in their minds, and as a result, they find themselves drifting through life, starting and stopping projects seemingly on a whim.

10

Goals

Once you have identified your Core Values and have crafted a Mission Statement, you will develop real-life goals that are expressions of your Core Values and Mission Statement. While Values are generally more abstract (e.g. Integrity, Service, Honesty, Love), *goals* are concrete ways of expressing these values.

I recommend that you develop concrete goals for all of the major areas of your life: physical goals (e.g. exercise three times per week, healthy diet), spiritual goals (e.g. read spiritual books, attend religious services, conquer a negative character trait), emotional goals (e.g. have more balanced mood and self-esteem), relationship goals (e.g. have a long-term relationship, spend more time with spouse and children) and professional goals (e.g. make a living doing something you love). Many experts recommend giving yourself a time-line for accomplishing these goals: three months, six months, twelve months, two years etc.

You will develop concrete goals for all of the major areas of your life:
physical goals, spiritual goals, emotional goals, relationship goals and professional goals.

Many people have been pursuing specific goals for many years, though they find themselves disconnected to these goals. This is often the result of having goals that are expressions of External Values rather than Core Values.

Ralph is a 42-year-old senior executive who reports that he is losing contact with his wife and two children, ages seven and eleven, due to being a "work-aholic." He acknowledged that he has given up nights and weekends with his family to continue climbing the corporate ladder. He reported feeling fatigued and unhappy with his life and his work productivity was beginning to suffer as well. He spent many hours working but found that he was often unproductive with his time. In my work with Ralph, he discovered that the External Value he was trying to satisfy was the value of Power. He told me that he had learned to covet this value from his father, a technology firm CEO. He also realized that he was giving up on a Core Value, namely Family. Ralph reflected on the fact that he was choosing an External Value (Power) over a Core Value (Family). While the pull to satisfy this External Value was very strong, Ralph slowly began shifting his energy to his value of Family and his relationship with his wife and children improved dramatically. He was even surprised to find that while he was not spending as much time as he used to at work, his time spent at work was becoming more productive and focused.

11

The Valued Self vs. The Narcissistic Self

When I begin working with clients on their self-evaluation system, I often hear a common fear from people who have had low self-esteem for many years. The concern sounds something like this: "But won't I become arrogant if I have high self-esteem?" To many people, the though of being arrogant is far worse than feeling crummy about themselves.

My response to them is that there is a difference between feeling a deep sense of value and being arrogant. We know this difference instinctually and we are drawn to those who possess the former and repulsed by those who display the latter. The difference is that the source of arrogance is a sense that one is better than others. This is certainly a repulsive stance to those who have to interact with this person. The reality is, that this stance is often just a defense against poor self-esteem. In order to heighten their sense of value, these people reduce others' value so they can feel good about themselves relative to their "inferior" neighbors.

A person with genuine self-worth on the other hand, feels no need to put others down in order to feel good about themselves. They must only make progress relative to their own values and life mission through the accomplishment of their goals. In fact, since many people contain the value of Service in their mission statement, their self-worth is actually elevated by making others feel good.

A person with genuine self-worth seems to be quietly saying to those around them "I am great, wonderful, splendid and powerful. And so are you!"

12

Anger

While anger can spur us to action at times when we feel too fearful or lethargic to act, in general, anger is rarely constructive. The prophets of old were said to lose their ability to connect to the divine source when in a state of anger. Researchers are finding evidence that many health problems are related to the extreme stress that stored anger places on our nervous system.

We know that we cannot connect to the ones we love when we are angry with them. So why do we get angry? The source of anger is rooted in the sense that life is not fair. On a deep level, we are not able to see any meaning in the pain of the situation. If we were able to see the meaning and personal growth potential inherent in every painful and difficult situation, our approach to pain in our lives would be different.

Once pain becomes linked with growth in our minds, we are able to face life with calm equanimity and a sense of purpose. Each challenge becomes an opportunity for deeper and deeper growth. I have found that the greatest growth happens when we are in a state of feeling connected to our purpose. This can happen even in the most difficult situations. Having clarity on the spiritual gain that is inherent to challenges shifts us to a state of spiritual pleasure. To do this, you must have clarity on your life purpose, and be able to see how everyday frustrations and larger scale problems can be used as stepping-stones to getting you closer to your goals.

There is an even deeper reason why people experience anger, and this reason is connected to our sense of value. Most of the time, we feel angry when others do not treat us with respect, whether they are family members, friends, coworkers or strangers. In essence, the root of our anger is that we feel devalued in these situations. Our psyche thinks "I can't let this person take away my value" and we are filled with rage that others have this kind of power over us. The remedy for this is an independent method of giving ourselves Value. If I feel value as a result of fulfilling my life purpose on a daily basis, then I will not be deeply affected by disrespect or any other negative messages from others. The reason most of us are so deeply affected by disrespect from others is that we are still really measuring our self worth based on others' opinions of us.

Our psyche thinks "I can't let this person take away my value" and we are filled with rage that others have this kind of power over us.

13

Integrating Your Life Mission

One of the best ways to integrate your life mission is to use it daily. What I mean by this is to check in with yourself multiple times a day with the question "how am I doing with my life mission?" If you assess that you are making progress, however small, you should give yourself a self-esteem point and feel good about this. If you are not moving forward, or are moving backwards, make a plan of small measurable goals to take in the next day, week and month and give yourself a self-esteem point for making this plan and following through with it. Like anything else in life, the more you practice this, the more it will become a reality for you. Be vigilant for the old ways of measuring yourself, and remind yourself that these self-measurements are not a part of your life mission.

Like anything else in life, the more you practice this, the more it will become a reality for you.

Mel is a single 36-year-old computer programmer who came to me with low self-esteem and anxiety issues. He stated that he has been judging himself by what others think of him for many years. As a result, he becomes very anxious in crowds, not knowing what others are thinking of him. In our work together, Mel recognized that his primary External Values were: Perfectionism and being perceived as perfect by others. He identified his Core Values as: Joy, Peace and Creativity. He then developed a mission statement to: "Spread joy, peace and creativity in the world." I encouraged him to have a conversation in his mind when he noticed his social anxiety creeping up. I instructed him to question the source of his anxiety and then remind himself of his Core Values. In the following session, he reported having the following mental conversation when he was late to a meeting:

> *"I am late to the meeting, I bet everyone is thinking that I am so irresponsible.*
>
> *What value am I judging myself with? The value of "having everyone think that I am perfect."*
>
> *Is this a Core Value or an External Value? This is an External Value that has nothing to do with my Core Values.*
>
> *What can I do to further my Core Values of joy, peace and creativity today? I will relax in this meeting and increase my inner peace, I will smile at my coworkers to increase their joy and I will work on giving at least one creative suggestion during the course of the meeting."*
>
> *Mel reported that as a result of this mental conversation, he started feeling more relaxed and happy almost immediately. He also felt that his self-esteem was raised as a result of making progress with his life mission.*

14

The Old Self-Measurements

Many of us find that the biggest challenge in being able to integrate our life mission into our thoughts and daily life, is the fact that we have measured ourselves for so many years using our old self-measurement standards. Many clients report to me that it feels like they have been wired to judge themselves according to their External Values. They question how they will be able to replace their old ineffective self-measurements with their life mission.

Much like learning to ride a bicycle becomes second nature after repeated practice, negative self-evaluations and the criteria we use to make our self-measurements, become hard-wired into our consciousness. In order to replace the old with the new, repeated use of one's Mission Statement is necessary. I encourage my clients to review their mission statement multiple times throughout the day. This accesses peoples' natural inclination to measure themselves, but this time, they are using the criteria that they have chosen.

Much like learning to ride a bicycle becomes second nature after repeated practice, negative self-evaluations become hard-wired into our consciousness.

With repeated practice, the use of new criteria for self-evaluation becomes second nature, while the old criteria start losing their power. Perseverance in this is the key. You are trying to rewire your neuro-connections, which research using thermal neuroimaging shows can be accomplished well into later years. The younger you are, the easier it will be as the brain is more elastic and old self-measurements have been hard-wired for a shorter period. It can be expected that old self-measurements will continue to intrude into one's consciousness during this work period, but it is well worth the effort to work through these. Instinctively, we all know that in order to achieve something worthwhile, there must be hard work. It will be helpful to remember that the reward for this work is a stable and lasting sense of self-worth. This in turn will serve as the foundation for physical, emotional, spiritual, relational and professional success for years to come.

15

The Integrated Self

Integration is the result of feeling comfortable with the often-conflicting parts of our self: the good, the bad, the generous and the selfish. Many people spend a great deal of their mental energy suppressing the parts of their selves that they feel are negative from their own consciousness. While this accomplishes the suppression of negative behaviors (i.e. we don't run around screaming like lunatics), it can also become the source of intense emotional turmoil. This is especially common in people who suppress their anger. Anger suppressors are so afraid of the harm they may cause if they release their anger that they place this anger far out of their conscious thoughts. If you ask them if they are angry, they would deny it. Over time, their anger may begin to surface as anxiety (fear of the catastrophe which their anger will cause if released) or depression, which is often the result of depleted mental energy being used up to suppress anger.

Many people spend a great deal of their mental energy suppressing the parts of their selves that they feel are negative from their own consciousness.

As a graduate student, we were instructed by a forensic psychology professor to imagine committing the most heinous crimes and to become comfortable with the parts of ourselves, which could commit these heinous acts. This was a technique this professor used to be able to understand the criminals she worked with. While acknowledging these parts of ourselves is never comfortable, being able to experience these parts (even if just in our own minds) releases all the energy required to suppress them and allows us to feel freer, lighter and more whole. We realize through this that what makes us good people is not that we do not have evil impulses, but that we choose to act in accordance with our higher selves despite our animal natures. The impact of full self-acceptance is far-reaching. We are able to become closer to people without the fear of being exposed, we feel more sane and comfortable with our internal conflicts and our health is promoted rather than jeopardized by the mental and physical stress of suppressed emotions.

> *William is a 19-year-old student who has been feeling depressed for a number of years. Through counseling, he discovered that he has been harboring intense feelings of anger towards his mother for remarrying and starting a new family. He recognized that he was afraid to acknowledge his anger, even to himself, because he was afraid he would lose his temper and ruin an already tenuous relationship with his mother. He also realized that his depression was the result of spending large amounts of mental energy trying to suppress his anger, leaving him emotionally exhausted and depressed. Through recognizing his anger and talking about his hurt feelings, William was able to appreciate that being angry was natural. Paradoxically, as he became more accepting of his anger and his depression subsided, he was able to make more of an effort to become closer to his mother.*

16

Insides vs. Outsides

One of the biggest benefits of changing your Self Evaluation System from an external system to an internal system is the amount of control this gives you. If I have to please multiple people in order to feel good about myself, I am at the mercy of others to feel good. On the other hand, if my evaluation system is based on internal processes that are under my control, then I will be able to feel good about myself no matter what others are thinking or saying.

I have found that many women are especially prone to accept physical beauty as their primary value source for self-esteem. This message is delivered by the media at a dizzying pace, and women need to be very clear on their own values to combat this. Since there is always someone more attractive, and they are always displayed on the cover of magazines for self-comparison purposes, most women feel they fall short. It is only after they have identified that this value has in fact taken hold and identified the values by which they truly value themselves that their personal power is restored.

If my evaluation system is based on internal processes that are under my control, then I will be able to feel good about myself, regardless of what others are thinking or saying.

17

Stay in the Process

After you have clarified your life purpose, make sure you focus on it as a process and not an end point. Many people get hung up on their life purpose as something that must be accomplished and completed in order to be enjoyed. I have found that this only leads to frustration. While a life purpose is never fully accomplished, no small amount of progress must get past your self-appreciation radar. Much like a painter enjoys the process of painting, you must enjoy the process of living out your life purpose. Focus on progress, no matter how small, and you will feel your Valued Self meter rise every day.

When you write out your mission statement, I encourage you to ask if this mission is process oriented or results oriented. Do you score points with yourself even if the end result does not turn out the way you want it to? If your value depends on the end result, you will most likely end up frustrated that you are not able to control the environment to bring about your desired outcome.

> *Stephanie is a 30-year-old beautician who is struggling with depression and low self-esteem. She identified her life mission as "to make others around me happy." She said that when others around her are unhappy, she does everything she can to "make them happy." She finds that she is often very frustrated by this. I pointed out to her that her mission is results oriented as opposed to process oriented. She scores a point with herself*

only when she "makes others happy." Since others are ultimately in control of their own happiness, she decided to change her mission to "use my skills and personality to work towards helping others become happier people." By recognizing that she can work towards helping others be happy instead of making people happy, she gained control over her value—she can always make an effort to help others.

18

Removing the Blocks

As a therapist, I have found that there are certain blocks that people have that get in the way of them being able to live their lives according to their identified life mission. The most common of these blocks is what cognitive-behavioral psychologists refer to as negative self-talk. These are the incessant, negative statements that we tell ourselves over and over which practically steal our self-esteem on a daily basis. The problem with negative self-talk is that we have been repeating these statements to ourselves over and over, thousands of times a day, and we no longer even notice them.

Much like a person who lives near an airport is able to tune out the noise after time, we tune out the noise that our minds are making. These negative statements hold us back and often tell us that we are not worthy of living out our life purpose. I recommend a period of journaling these thoughts for a couple of weeks to begin to identify these thoughts and to become more aware of them as they arise. The next step is learning to talk back to these thoughts, which having a clear life purpose allows you to do.

The problem with negative self-talk is that we have been repeating these statements to ourselves over and over, thousands of times a day. We no longer even notice that they are there.

19

Cognitive-Behavioral Therapy (CBT)

The most widely used method in psychology for learning to reprogram negative self-talk is known as Cognitive-Behavioral Therapy (CBT). The essence of CBT is the following lesson: it is not external events that cause us to experience an emotional reaction, rather it is the way we perceive these events that matters. For example: two people may be caught in the same traffic jam. One person is thinking "this is a disaster, I am going to be late, get fired and be homeless." Naturally, this person will feel panic. The other person thinks "there is nothing I can do about this, I will be late for work but these things happen. I am sure it will be fine. I can have some time to myself and listen to music." This person will be feeling calm. Their thoughts are controlling their emotions—not the traffic jam.

Learning to manage negative self-talk will make following through with your dreams and discovering your Valued Self much easier.

CBT aims at helping people become aware of the thoughts and beliefs that keep them scared and depressed. Once they become aware of them, the next step is to reprogram them to become more realistic. This process is relevant to the Valued Self process because many people allow their negative self-talk to sabotage their life mission and goals. They tell themselves things like "this will never work," and "I will fail" etc. The primary way to begin working on these thoughts is what CBT refers to as ABC worksheets. Taking a sheet of paper, divide the sheet into three columns. Write A above the left column, B above the middle column and C above the right column. "A" stands for Activating Event, it is the event that triggers your thoughts and emotions. For example: the traffic jam. "B" stands for Beliefs and these are the thoughts that run through your mind as a result of the event. For example: "I am going to get fired." "C" stands for emotional Consequence, and this is what you feel as a result of what you think. For example: panic.

I instruct my patients to fill out one of these sheets per day. Most people struggle with identifying what they were thinking at the time of the event, but the ability to do so develops with practice. I suggest this exercise be completed as close to possible directly following an event that triggered strong emotions. The next step is to begin looking at the B column and asking yourself if these thoughts are realistic. If they are not realistic, then practice thinking what you will tell yourself if this comes up again in the future. Learning to manage negative self-talk will make following through with your dreams and discovering your Valued Self much easier.

20

Taking Back Projections

Projections are beliefs from our past that we use to interpret our present. These beliefs serve as a map that we use to understand life experiences, the world, other people and ourselves. For example: if as a child you had a mean teacher with a strong personality, you may instinctively dislike people with strong personalities as an adult.

The projections we have about ourselves are directly related to our sense of Self. These beliefs are often very limiting beliefs which we have about ourselves and which we subconsciously project outwards. For instance, if you believe you are worthy of being valued by others, you will non-verbally send out messages to others that you are worthy of value. The opposite is also true, others pick up messages from us that we are not worthy of being valued and they treat us accordingly.

Being aware of the way you are projecting your old values on others and how they project their values on you will help you catch yourself from falling into their trap.

The reason we do this is something called congruence: the need to have our insides match our outsides. If we feel that others are valuing us and we do not feel we deserve this, we often find ways to convince others that we are not valuable. The instinct to do this is especially strong for people who are working on resetting their self-value system from externally based to internally based values. In order to successfully reset your Values, you will have to repeatedly resist the urge to go back to following your External Value System. You will have to consistently focus on your Core Values and Mission Statement and evaluate yourself based on these, until they become natural.

A major challenge arises for people when they are working on resetting their values and people who have known them for years continue to devalue them or try to influence them to go back to using their old value system. Being aware of the way you are projecting your old values to others and how they project their values on you will help you catch yourself from falling into their trap.

21

True Self vs. False Self

Years ago, I was a participant in an intensive group process workshop for men. The men in this group were working on achieving their full potential and we would focus the entire group focus on one specific participant at a time. I remember how uncomfortable it felt to be in the "hot seat" and have the entire group focus their attention on me and offer me feedback on my personality, interpersonal interactions, life goals etc.

One particular participant was a young man, about the same age as myself, who appeared perfectly comfortable with having the group focus their attention on him. He smiled coolly throughout the entire process and gently accepted the feedback he was given. At one point, another participant stated: "It seems like your face is a mask for what you are really feeling." Many other group members began to acknowledge that they agreed with this comment and this man's face slowly changed from smiling to crying. After a few minutes he said that he had worn this mask since he was a young child when he was very shy and felt isolated from his peers. He said that he made a decision from a young age to always smile, even when he was unhappy.

At one point, another participant stated: "It seems like your face is a mask for what you are really feeling."

In psychological terms, this young man had developed a False Self. This is a social self that is developed for adaptive purposes and serves as a defensive mechanism. It is a way of concealing the True Self, which may have some components that are undesirable. The cost of having a rigid False Self and denying one's True Self is a sense of feeling disconnected from one's inner reality, as well as emotional exhaustion caused by the effort it takes to repress one's true thoughts, feelings and personality.

I often recommend that people experiment with letting their True Selves emerge gradually and test the waters with it. Many people believe that others will not accept their True Selves and they fear that this will impact their sense of value. Working on changing your self-measurement values to be consistent with who you are and want to be, rather than what others want from you, will help you become more connected with your True Self. This process is known as changing the *locus of control* from an external source (other's judgments) to an internal source (your Core Values).

Many anxiety disorders are actually the result of having an external locus of control. For example, I work with a client who himself is an excellent financial consultant. Unfortunately, his fears have held him back from fully realizing his potential. He worries that others will reject his ideas and that he will be labeled a failure. This worry holds him back from expressing many of his original ideas. Thorough our work together he was able to make an important shift. While he previously measured success on whether or not his ideas were accepted by others, we worked on having him measure success in regards to the effort he put into his work. Through shifting his value paradigm from the external value of approval to the internal value of effort, he was able to overcome his anxiety of failing.

22

The Valued Marriage

In my work with couples, I have found a consistent pattern of conflict. Partners appear to be struggling with each other for a sense value. Partners who deeply value each other and express that value openly and often, tend to be happy and healthy. When one partner wants something from the other, it is usually in an area that makes them feel valued by the other. While marriage should be the ultimate haven of mutual value and appreciation, our subconscious often forces us to be attracted to people who will challenge that sense of value at it's core. We tend to seek out partners who will return us to the scene of childhood where we felt least valued, thereby repeating the past.

Partners who deeply value each other and express that value openly and often, tend to be happy and healthy.

We do this because our subconscious mind wants to fix this childhood wound. Imago Therapy, developed by Dr. Harville Hendrix, focuses on helping partners heal childhood wounds with each other. What complicates this process is the fact that it is largely subconscious; most people do not realize that they are seeking to be restored to a sense of value by their partner. The problem is that when you do not have the means of filling up your own self-esteem meter, your partner feels burdened by the responsibility of boosting your self-esteem. Once partners start to become responsible for their own self-esteem they find that the areas of conflict tend to decrease dramatically.

23

The Valued Parent

One of the greatest gifts parents can give their child is to have parents with healthy senses of self. Children who see their parents valuing themselves learn the valuable lesson that they too are valuable. Parents who feel that their life has purpose and direction tend to be more emotionally available to their children. When a parent's self-esteem meter is full, they have positive energy to share with their children. When a parent's self-esteem meter is low, they are more easily irritated and have little warmth and positive energy to share.

Children who see their parents valuing themselves learn the valuable lesson that they too are valuable.

Since children cannot understand that their parent's unhappiness is not their fault, they assume that the reason their parent is unhappy is because of them. Children feel guilty for this and will expend endless amounts of energy to try to help their parent. This process reverses the healthy roles of parent and child and can take away the happiness that children need to experience in order to thrive as adults.

Parents often tell me that they feel guilty pursuing their own dreams because this may take time away from their family. I often share with them a standard safety procedure which airlines have been teaching us for decades: Parents must place the oxygen mask on themselves before they place it over their children. The reasoning is simple. If you pass out, you will be jeopardizing yourself and your child. You must take care of yourself in order to have what to give others and this includes your children. Giving to yourself is not selfish—it is the only way to have something to share. Focusing on your personal life purpose will make you a happy and fulfilled adult who will have the gift of your full personality and energy to share with your loved ones.

24

Teenagers and Twentysomethings

Teenagers and twentysomethings are increasingly finding themselves at a loss for a sense of purpose and direction in their lives. Whereas in previous times a bachelors degree was more than enough to start a career, young people are now expected to get a masters degree or doctorate to be competitive. These new education standards have pushed the age of maturity forward and being twenty-five and living at home is no longer unusual.

Teens and twentysomethings are now spending years in a process of "finding themselves" that leads them to mountaintops and across the world looking for meaning. The positive side effect of this is that these young people have an opportunity that their parents did not. With the requirement to enter the workforce significantly delayed, young adults can spend the time to discover their true inner values and selves, something their parents never had the luxury of doing.

The primary questions at this age are "what do I want in life" and "what do I have to do to be valued by my peers?" While this stage may be frustrating for parents, successful parents will nurture this process without trying to impose their values and goals on their young-adult children. If you have ever been the recipient of unsolicited advice then you know how ineffective it is. I suggest that parents resist the urge to give their children unsolicited advice. At the same time, cultivating an open, respectful and trusting relationship with your teen and twentysomething will allow them the option of coming to you for advice when they are ready for it.

The primary questions at this age are "what do I want in life?" and "What do I have to do be valued by my peers?"

Parents also must realize that they will likely not succeed in being their children's life coach or therapist. Young adults at this age are far too invested in creating space between themselves and their parents. Doing so, allows them to begin feeling a sense of independence. Parents who are comfortable with their young adult child's need to distance and differentiate themselves will allow the Valued Self process to unfold. Once the young-adult has asserted their independence and sees that the parent is not fighting this process, a natural return to the child-parent bond can be expected.

25

The Valued Child

Child psychologists have identified the ideal environment for children to be raised: *an environment in which the child feels inherently valued.* Despite this, many parents fear that too much positive reinforcement will spoil their children. They are concerned that their children will never learn how to change their behaviors and mature unless they are guided through criticism, and this is not unrealistic. The reality is that children do need boundaries and children rely on their parents for guidance. There is a delicate balance between giving your children what Carl Rogers referred to as *unconditional positive regard* and letting your children think anything goes. As a result, psychologists have devised the following formula: constructive criticism is allowed and even desirable, but in order to maintain a Value-enhancing environment, it must be offset by five times as many positive and reaffirming comments. Again, that is a 5:1 ratio of positive to critical experiences.

There is a neurochemical reason for this: the reptilian brain is programmed to flee from pain and move towards pleasure. When interactions with parents are mostly positive, the relationship is cemented through a natural tendency to desire closeness. Unfortunately, many parent-child relationships are centered on criticism and the natural reaction develops into one of fight or flight. The solution is to change the relationship to a consistent exchange of positive interactions. While it may not seem natural at first, it will literally transform the quality of your relationships with your children. Remember that the essential desire of young children is to feel valued by their parents.

Exceptional parenting happens when parents are attuned to their children's strengths and interests. When a parent values these parts of the child, the child's Valued Self begins to emerge and solidify. The experience of being valued for who they really are sets a very strong foundation for lifelong healthy self-esteem.

The experience of being valued for who they really are sets a very strong foundation for lifelong healthy self-esteem.

26

The Valued Self and Aging

Many people spend their entire lives feeling happy and fulfilled and notice that all of this changes when they become old or ill. The reason for this is often that their source of value comes under attack when they become physically limited.

> *Robert is a 72-year-old man who has been clinically depressed since he had a heart attack and had to stop all of the physical activities that he defined himself by. Sadly, he became so depressed that he felt his life had no purpose. Our work together focused on helping him redefine his purpose and values. He came to realize that his true values were in the areas of family and service to others. He was then able to make goals that reflected these values and begin the process of reengaging in a meaningful and enjoyable lifestyle.*

While nobody wants to become limited, life sometimes challenges us to discover what is really important to us. Our society tends to value productivity. Those who are older or ill may not be able to be as productive and their sense of self often suffers. On the other hand, a person who has defined their Core Values will find opportunities to "score value points" in many different ways. What is needed is the resourcefulness to adapt their Core Values to whatever life situation they find themselves in.

For example, if service to others is a Core Value for you, you will find ways to be of service even in difficult situations. When an uncle of mine was sick in the hospital, he always made sure to smile and joke with the nurses who told us that he always brightened their day. My uncle was able to express and grow his Valued Self even when he was lying in a bed and dependent on others for his most basic needs.

27

The Valued Self and Image

Many of us have internalized the External Values of thinness and physical beauty as defined by our society as part of our Self Evaluation System. Research has shown that strangers perceive heavier people as less intelligent and capable than thin people as a result of these societal standards. Many of my overweight patients report feeling that they feel little or no self-value as a result of their weight. They in turn find themselves feeling depressed. The more depressed they get, the more they eat to drown their depression, and the cycle continues. When eating becomes reinforced as the way to handle emotional pain, this cycle becomes an almost insurmountable obstacle, and the more it is repeated, the harder a habit it becomes to break.

My approach to this problem is to attack the problem at it's root. I suggest that patients clarify their self-evaluation system. Do they want to measure themselves based on their weight? Do they feel this way of measuring themselves will help them meet their goals as a human being? I often ask "What do you want written on your gravestone?" How about "Here lies Joe Smith, he was a thin man" or "Here lies Tracy Wells, Size 2." Most of us want something like "Here lies Jacob Evans, beloved father and husband, a giving spirit and trusted friend." This is the true test of your Core Values. Knowing what you want to contribute and what you want to be remembered for will clarify what you should spend the rest of your life working on. It will also clarify what standards you should spend the rest of your life measuring yourself with.

Knowing what you want to contribute will clarify what you should spend the rest of your life working on.

The only reason to measure yourself at all is because measuring yourself will help you achieve your goals. It will let you know how you are doing with your life mission, if you are you making progress or not. All other types of self-judgment are usually harmful or irrelevant at best. Judging yourself negatively based on your weight when it is not a Core Value is also harmful. On the other hand, many of us have physical health as a Core Value. You will notice a big difference between the negative self-talk of a person who values health over physical beauty. Most people berate themselves very harshly when it comes to their not meeting their physical beauty standards. On the other hand, we tend to be quite kind with ourselves when we are considering if the choices we are about to make are healthy or not. The reason for this distinction is that the former is accessing our External Values while the later is accessing our Internal (Core) Values. When you begin to connect with your Core Values, you will find that the cycle of berating yourself, becoming depressed and overeating stops.

28

The Valued Self and Spirituality

The realm of spirituality has historically intersected with psychology in a very profound way: While spirituality taught man how to live, psychology helped man remove the blocks from getting there. After years of psychotherapy, many patients find themselves with the following problem: "I no longer hate my parents, now what?" These people are now faced with the question of what to do with their lives now that the emotional blocks formed in childhood have been overcome. While religion may not be for everyone, spirituality appears to be universal. Yoga, meditational practices, backpacking missions in search of spiritual wisdom have all become the norm. The paradox for many young men and women who seek meaning in their lives is that when they return from their travels, the report is often the same: "the answer was within me all along." The search for meaning is really a search for self. It is a search for that meaning which will define the self and nurture it for a lifetime.

The search for meaning is really a search for self. It is a search for that meaning which will define the self and nurture it for a lifetime.

29

The Valued Self and Suffering

As Viktor Frankl aptly put it: Man will endure any amount of suffering when he sees meaning in it. People who have identified their life purpose are able to navigate the storms of life with equanimity. They know that what matters most is always available to them—to further their life mission and contribution to humanity. Their self is defined not by how pleasant their lives are, but by how they engage the situations which life places them in. Life is full of pain, in fact, pain is the price we pay for growth. When pain is seen as senseless, it turns into suffering. When pain is seen as meaningful, it turns into a catalyst for greatness. Think of the people who you truly respect. Does the fact that they have overcome difficulty have anything to do with your respect for them? Finding ways to connect the pain in your life to your life mission will build your Valued Self in ways that comfort never could.

....

Man will endure any amount of suffering when he sees meaning in it.

-Viktor Frankl

....

30

The Benefits of a Valued Self

Research has already shown us multiple examples of the powerful connection between the body and mind. When the mind is stressed, the body tends to become ill. People with mental health concerns have higher incidence rates of numerous health problems including increased risk for heart disease. As I mentioned earlier in the book, Dr. Gardner, the renowned child psychologist, found that despite the many variations of problems he saw in the children he treated, every single one of those children was there primarily for self-esteem problems.

Adults are no different: the myriad of self defeating behaviors which adults with low self-esteem exhibit is living proof of this. One of my favorite outgrowths of healthy, self-defined self-esteem is the freedom that it provides from others' judgments of us. How many people find themselves held back from fully expressing themselves and pursuing their deepest happiness because they fear negative evaluation from others? How many of us are afraid to speak up for what we want out of concern for what negative feedback this may illicit? A person who is clear of what their values and what their specific life goals are, is truly free to act as he wishes, speak as he wishes and live life being fully present to every experience as it unfolds.

My hope for you is that you will discover and unleash your Valued Self and that you will live a life full of happiness, purpose and connection.

PART II

The Valued Self

Workbook©

1

Overview—The Valued Self Method in Five Steps

- Pre-test. Before you begin the Five Steps, you will use a standardized scale to get a baseline measurement of your self-esteem before you reset your self-worth values. You will be able to use this scale to measure your progress as you progress.
- Step 1—*Identify Your Self Evaluation System.* Here you will take an honest accounting of all the different criteria that you use to measure your self-worth. They will likely be a combination of your true values, or Core Values, and values that you perceive others (including society) expect from you or value you for, or External Values.
- Step 2—*Identify your Core Values.* You will differentiate between your External Values and Core Values in your Self Evaluation System. You will also add additional ideal Core Values to your Core Values System that are not yet part of your Self Evaluation System.
- Step 3—*The Mission Statement.* You will craft your Core Values into a Mission Statement that encompasses these Core Values. This will be an aspirational statement that describes what you want to accomplish with your life. It will guide your decisions depending on whether the choice in front of you adds or detracts from your life mission. Through repeatedly using this mission as the standard by which you measure yourself by, you will develop your Valued Self. External Values and judgments will begin to hold little to no power over you as you integrate

this mission into your thinking and allow it to become your primary guide in life.

- Step 4—*Goal Setting.* The next step is to explore real ways to express and fulfill your mission in your life. This means making a list of concrete goals in all areas of your life that will be connected to and inspired by your life mission.
- Step 5—*Identifying and Removing Blocks.* The final step is to discover the reasons and life factors that are getting in the way of fulfilling this mission and expressing it in life through your goals. These blocks can be environmental (poor social support, negative relationships, finances) or psychological (negative self-talk, harsh self-criticism, projections from your past). Negative self-talk is worked on in this stage to make our self-statements more in line with our life mission. Many people have found working with a therapist or life coach most helpful for this stage.
- Post-Test—At any point in the Five Step process you may measure your progress with the Rosenberg Self-Esteem Scale again to see how The Valued Self Method has impacted your self-esteem. Continue to use this scale in the weeks to come as you make use of your Mission Statement and fulfill your goals.

2

The Valued Self Principles

1. Healthy self-esteem is achieved when we clarify our core values and learn to evaluate ourselves exclusively by these standards.
2. We learn to measure ourselves in terms of our effort and progress towards our mission and credit ourselves for every step forward which we make.
3. We learn to disregard values that are not relevant to our core values. This gives us the freedom to be ourselves.
4. Once we have identified our core values, we will develop a mission statement for our life that expresses our core values. We will further develop real-life goals that express our life mission in the world. We will spend the rest of lives working to express this mission.
5. Though this mission is a lifelong process, our lives will be filled with value in its pursuit.

3

Pre-Test: Get a Baseline

Use the scale below to measure your baseline self-esteem. You will measure your self-esteem again when you complete this workbook.

Instructions: Below is a list of statements dealing with your general feelings about yourself. If you strongly agree, circle **SA**. If you agree with the statement, circle **A**. If you disagree, circle **D**. If you strongly disagree, circle **SD**.

1.	On the whole, I am satisfied with myself.	SA (3)	A (2)	D (1)	SD (0)
2.	At times, I think I am no good at all.	SA (0)	A (1)	D (2)	SD (3)
3.	I feel that I have a number of good qualities.	SA (3)	A (2)	D (1)	SD (0)
4.	I am able to do things as well as most other people.	SA (3)	A (2)	D (1)	SD (0)
5.	I feel I do not have much to be proud of.	SA (0)	A (1)	D (2)	SD (3)
6.	I certainly feel useless at times.	SA (0)	A (1)	D (2)	SD (3)
7.	I feel that I'm a person of worth, at least on an equal plane with others.	SA (3)	A (2)	D (1)	SD (0)
8.	I wish I could have more respect for myself.	SA (0)	A (1)	D (2)	SD (3)

		SA	A	D	SD
9.	All in all, I am inclined to feel that I am a failure.	SA (0)	A (1)	D (2)	SD (3)
10.	I take a positive attitude toward myself.	SA (3)	A (2)	D (1)	SD (0)

Scoring: 15-25 = Normal Range

My score: ________________

Rosenberg Self-Esteem Scale (Rosenberg, 1989)

4

Step 1: The Self Evaluation System

Self-esteem is the result of how you measure yourself. It is important for you to clarify all of the standards that your self-assessment system includes. Think about your friends, family, coworkers, your religion, your work environment, your finances, your health, your looks, what strangers think of you. All of these and more may be components of your Self Evaluation System (SES).

My Self Evaluation System (SES) includes:

1. ______________________________
2. ______________________________
3. ______________________________
4. ______________________________
5. ______________________________
6. ______________________________
7. ______________________________
8. ______________________________
9. ______________________________
10. ______________________________

5

Step 2: Core Values

Identify all of the values that are truly important and meaningful to you regardless of what others may think or say about these. These are your Core Values.

1. ______________________________
2. ______________________________
3. ______________________________
4. ______________________________
5. ______________________________
6. ______________________________
7. ______________________________
8. ______________________________
9. ______________________________

Compare these values to the values in Step 1. Place a check mark next the items in Step 1 that are compatible with your core values. Place an X mark next to those that are not compatible with your core values.

6

Step 3: Mission Statement

Create a Mission Statement that summarizes your key core values into one or two statements.

My mission in life is to:

1.____

____

____.

____

Notes:

7

Step 4: Goal Setting

Identify goals in all of the below areas which are real life expressions of your life mission:

Physical Goals: Notes:

1.____________________ ____________________

2.____________________ ____________________

3.____________________ ____________________

Spiritual Goals:

1.____________________ ____________________

2.____________________ ____________________

3.____________________ ____________________

Emotional Goals:

1.____________________ ____________________

2.____________________ ____________________

3.____________________ ____________________

Relationship Goals:

1.____________________ ____________________

2.____________________ ____________________

3____________________ ____________________

Professional Goals:

1.______________________________ ______________________________

2.______________________________ ______________________________

8

Step 5: Removing Blocks

Thinking ahead, what will make accomplishing your goals difficult? Make sure to include External Values that have a strong negative impact on you when you do not satisfy their demands. What do you tell yourself at these times? Work through this negative self-talk using journaling, Cognitive-Behavioral Therapy (See chapter 19 and the bestseller "Feeling Good" by Dr. David Burns), talking to a close friend or family member about these, or making use of a coach or counselor. This is the area where the most difficult and worthwhile self-growth occurs. It requires patience and perseverance and is well worth the effort.

List your "Blocks:"

1.____
2.____
3.____

What are some ways you can work on removing these blocks:

1.____
2.____
3.____

9

Post-Test: Measure Your Progress

After a period of assessing your progress based on your life mission and disregarding external judgments that are not compatible or relevant to your life mission, reassess your self-esteem.

Instructions: Below is a list of statements dealing with your general feelings about yourself. If you strongly agree, circle **SA**. If you agree with the statement, circle **A**. If you disagree, circle **D**. If you strongly disagree, circle **SD**.

1.	On the whole, I am satisfied with myself.	SA (3)	A (2)	D (1)	SD (0)
2.	At times, I think I am no good at all.	SA (0)	A (1)	D (2)	SD (3)
3.	I feel that I have a number of good qualities.	SA (3)	A (2)	D (1)	SD (0)
4.	I am able to do things as well as most other people.	SA (3)	A (2)	D (1)	SD (0)
5.	I feel I do not have much to be proud of.	SA (0)	A (1)	D (2)	SD (3)
6.	I certainly feel useless at times.	SA (0)	A (1)	D (2)	SD (3)
7.	I feel that I'm a person of worth, at least on an equal plane with others.	SA (3)	A (2)	D (1)	SD (0)
8.	I wish I could have more respect for myself.	SA (0)	A (1)	D (2)	SD (3)

		SA	A	D	SD
9.	All in all, I am inclined to feel that I am a failure.	SA (0)	A (1)	D (2)	SD (3)
10.	I take a positive attitude toward myself.	SA (3)	A (2)	D (1)	SD (0)

Scoring: 15-25 = Normal Range

My score: ____________________

Rosenberg Self-Esteem Scale (Rosenberg, 1989)

PART III

The Valued Self©

Appendices

Appendix A

The Valued Self Method—A Technical Overview

The Valued Self Method has five components, with a pretest and posttest at the beginning and end of the process. Before beginning the Five Steps to a Valued Self, we measure your self-esteem using a self-report scale known as the Rosenberg Self-Esteem Scale (1965). This gives us a baseline to help us track your progress. After the baseline is determined, Step 1 is to take a full accounting of all of the criteria, standards and values that you currently use to measure yourself with. I call this your Self Evaluation System (SES). It will include values from two categories: a. Core Values—these are values which are meaningful to you and which further your sense of life purpose and meaning and b. External Values—these are values which are external to your life purpose and which are either irrelevant or in conflict with your Core Values.

Until this point, there has been no distinction in your self-evaluation system. You have unconsciously valued yourself based on both Core Values and External Values. Since these two categories are often in conflict, most people have experienced a significant amount of inner turmoil, confusion and unstable self-esteem. For example, a person may have "being a spiritual person" as a Core Value and "being famous" as an External Value. This person will thus experience a significant amount of internal conflict when a decision arises that requires her to do something that is not in line with her spirituality in order for her to become famous.

Next (Step 2), we work to differentiate the values included in your Self Evaluation System into Core Values and External Values. This step also identifies latent Core Values that you have not yet become conscious of. The combination of your current Core Values and these newly identified Core Values make up your Core Value System (CVS). Clarifying your External Values, i.e. those values that are in conflict or irrelevant to your Core Values, helps with continuing to make the distinction between Core Values and External Values as they arise in your daily life. The goal of the Valued Self Method is to have you living a life that is governed only by your Core Values. To assist with this, (Step 3) the Core Values are crafted into a Mission Statement, which encompasses your Core Values. This Mission Statement is then used as a guide to live by.

In Step 4, real life goals are identified in every area of one's life (physical, spiritual, emotional, relational and professional) that reflects this life mission. Self-esteem points are then accrued internally when action is taken towards fulfilling these goals. The focus of Step 5 is using techniques to further the internal work of combating self-criticisms which arise as a result of not fulfilling External Values which are now considered irrelevant or in conflict with one's life purpose. When this is not done, people often feel like there is a hole in the bottom of their self-esteem boat—no matter how hard they work on their mission, their self-esteem remains low. I refer to this as one's Blocks—the pull one feels from External Values that have been used for self-criticism for years and years. In this step, tools from this book, including Cognitive-Behavioral Therapy (CBT), are used to remove these blocks. Finally, we again use the Rosenberg Self-Esteem Scale to measure your progress.

Interested parties may contact the author regarding research conducted on Value Processing Therapy (VPT) as this is an ongoing project.

Appendix B

List of Values

This list is designed to help you reach a better understanding of your most significant values. You will notice that this is a very long list. Much like there are many foods to match the varied tastes of people, so too there are many values which speak differently to each of us in different ways. You will also notice that this list includes values that are both common Core Values (Service to others, Family etc.) and common External Values (Power, Recognition etc.). Recognizing both of these types of values in your Self Evaluation System is the key to developing a Valued Self.

1. Abundance
2. Acceptance
3. Accomplishment
4. Accuracy
5. Achievement
6. Acknowledgement
7. Activeness
8. Adaptability
9. Adoration
10. Adventure
11. Affection
12. Affluence
13. Aggressiveness
14. Agility
15. Alertness
16. Altruism

17. Ambition
18. Amusement
19. Anticipation
20. Appreciation
21. Approachability
22. Articulacy
23. Assertiveness
24. Attentiveness
25. Attractiveness
26. Audacity
27. Availability
28. Awareness
29. Awe
30. Balance
31. Beauty
32. Being the best
33. Belonging
34. Benevolence
35. Bliss
36. Boldness
37. Bravery
38. Brilliance
39. Calmness
40. Camaraderie/ Having friends
41. Caring for others
42. Carefulness
43. Celebrity
44. Certainty
45. Challenge
46. Charity
47. Charm
48. Chastity
49. Cheerfulness
50. Clarity
51. Cleanliness
52. Clear-mindedness

53. Cleverness
54. Closeness
55. Comfort
56. Commitment
57. Compassion
58. Competence
59. Completion
60. Composure
61. Concentration
62. Confidence
63. Conformity
64. Congruency (Having your outsides match your insides)
65. Connection
66. Consciousness
67. Consistency
68. Contentment
69. Continuity
70. Contribution
71. Control
72. Conviction
73. Coolness
74. Cooperation
75. Correctness
76. Courage
77. Courtesy
78. Craftiness
79. Creativity
80. Credibility
81. Cunning
82. Curiosity
83. Daring
84. Decisiveness
85. Decorum
86. Deference
87. Delight
88. Dependability

89. Depth
90. Desire
91. Determination
92. Devotion
93. Devoutness
94. Dexterity
95. Dignity
96. Diligence
97. Direction
98. Directness
99. Discipline
100. Discovery
101. Discretion
102. Diversity
103. Dominance
104. Dreaming
105. Drive
106. Duty
107. Dynamism
108. Eagerness
109. Economy
110. Ecstasy
111. Education
112. Effectiveness
113. Efficiency
114. Elation
115. Elegance
116. Empathy
117. Encouragement
118. Endurance
119. Energy
120. Enjoyment
121. Entertainment
122. Enthusiasm
123. Excellence
124. Excitement

125. Exhilaration
126. Expectancy
127. Expediency
128. Experience
129. Expertise
130. Exploration
131. Expressiveness
132. Extravagance
133. Extroversion
134. Exuberance
135. Fairness
136. Faith
137. Fame
138. Family
139. Fascination
140. Fashion
141. Fearlessness
142. Ferocity
143. Fidelity
144. Fierceness
145. Financial independence
146. Firmness
147. Fitness
148. Flexibility
149. Flow
150. Fluency
151. Focus
152. Fortitude
153. Frankness
154. Freedom
155. Friendliness
156. Frugality
157. Fun
158. Gallantry
159. Generosity
160. Giving

161. Grace
162. Gratitude
163. Gregariousness
164. Growth
165. Guidance
166. Happiness
167. Harmony
168. Health
169. Heart
170. Helpfulness
171. Heroism
172. Holiness
173. Honesty
174. Honor
175. Hopefulness
176. Hospitality
177. Humility
178. Humor
179. Hygiene
180. Imagination
181. Impact
182. Impartiality
183. Independence
184. Industry
185. Ingenuity
186. Inquisitiveness
187. Insightfulness
188. Inspiration
189. Integrity
190. Intelligence
191. Intensity
192. Intimacy
193. Introversion
194. Intuition
195. Intuitiveness
196. Inventiveness

197. Joy
198. Judiciousness
199. Justice
200. Kindness
201. Knowledge
202. Leadership
203. Learning
204. Liberty
205. Liveliness
206. Logic
207. Longevity
208. Love
209. Loyalty
210. Majesty
211. Making a difference
212. Mastery
213. Maturity
214. Meekness
215. Mellowness
216. Meticulousness
217. Mindfulness
218. Modesty
219. Motivation
220. Mysteriousness
221. Neatness
222. Nerve
223. Obedience
224. Open-mindedness
225. Openness
226. Optimism
227. Order
228. Organization
229. Originality
230. Outlandishness
231. Outrageousness
232. Passion

233. Peace
234. Perceptiveness
235. Perfection
236. Perkiness
237. Perseverance
238. Persistence
239. Persuasiveness
240. Philanthropy
241. Piety
242. Playfulness
243. Pleasantness
244. Pleasure
245. Poise
246. Popularity
247. Power
248. Practicality
249. Precision
250. Preparedness
251. Presence
252. Privacy
253. Proactivity
254. Professionalism
255. Prosperity
256. Prudence
257. Punctuality
258. Purity
259. Realism
260. Reason
261. Reasonableness
262. Recognition
263. Recreation
264. Refinement
265. Reflection
266. Relaxation
267. Reliability
268. Religiousness

269. Resilience
270. Resolution
271. Resolve
272. Resourcefulness
273. Respect
274. Rest
275. Restraint
276. Reverence
277. Richness
278. Rigor
279. Sacredness
280. Sacrifice
281. Saintliness
282. Satisfaction
283. Security
284. Self-control
285. Self-esteem
286. Selflessness
287. Self-reliance
288. Sensitivity
289. Sensuality
290. Serenity
291. Service
292. Sexuality
293. Sharing
294. Shrewdness
295. Significance
296. Silence
297. Silliness
298. Simplicity
299. Sincerity
300. Skillfulness
301. Solidarity
302. Solitude
303. Soundness
304. Speed

305. Spirit
306. Spirituality
307. Spontaneity
308. Spunk
309. Stability
310. Stealth
311. Stillness
312. Strength
313. Structure
314. Success
315. Support
316. Supremacy
317. Surprise
318. Sympathy
319. Synergy
320. Teamwork
321. Thankfulness
322. Thoroughness
323. Thoughtfulness
324. Thrift
325. Tidiness
326. Timeliness
327. Traditionalism
328. Tranquility
329. Transcendence
330. Trust
331. Trustworthiness
332. Truth
333. Understanding
334. Unflappability
335. Uniqueness
336. Unity
337. Usefulness
338. Utility

339. Valor
340. Variety
341. Victory
342. Vigor
343. Virtue
344. Vision
345. Vitality
346. Vivacity
347. Warmth
348. Watchfulness
349. Wealth
350. Willfulness
351. Willingness
352. Winning
353. Wisdom
354. Wittiness
355. Wonder
356. Youthfulness
374. Zeal

Appendix C

Sample Mission Statements

- To motivate, educate, and inspire others to be their best through my writing and speaking.
- To raise happy, healthy, well-adjusted children and grand children by listening to their needs and teaching them to be self-sufficient.
- Bring the level of customer service in my company to an all-time high and keep it going so that the company grows by at least 10 percent annually.
- Help the broke, lonely, down-trodden, desperate people of this world see that there is hope. To help them get on their feet and live respectable lives.
- Lead my community in becoming a better place for its citizens. To have better schools, better homes, better lives and brighter futures. To bring in companies that can provide jobs and increase the standard of living for all families.
- Use my talents and skills to help others live healthier lives.
- Help teenagers believe in themselves and help them develop their God-given talents.
- Volunteer my time, talents, and resources to provide development opportunities for disadvantaged children.
- Accomplish excellence in whatever endeavor I choose for my life.
- To use my education and experience to motivate others to want better oral hygiene for themselves and their families.

- To make a difference in my community by selectively giving some of my earnings to those in need.
- To achieve what matters most. To help others do the same.

Appendix D

How to Write Your Personal Mission Statement

One of the greatest gifts you can give yourself is to write a personal mission statement. Why? Because when you're faced with a difficult choice to make, choosing the option that fits with your purpose in life will be easier if you have a mission statement to reference. Also, your mission statement will (should) motivate you. Allow me to explain further.

A mission statement describes your unique purpose in life. It summarizes the talents and qualities you have and want to develop, what you want to accomplish, and what contributions you desire to make.

What are you passionate about? What really excites you? What would make you jump out of bed in the morning knowing that if you didn't show up it would make a huge difference in the cause?

Passion is so important when creating your mission statement. If you're not passionate about your mission, it's not really your mission. If it doesn't speak to your soul and keep you awake at night thinking about the possibilities, you haven't hit on the right thing yet.

While the specifics of how you fulfill your mission may come in stages, your mission will more than likely remain the same throughout your lifetime. Even though you play different roles during different phases of your life, one thing will always remain constant—your mission.

Having a personal mission statement helps you make daily decisions. When you have a choice to make, which option gets you closer to accomplishing your ultimate goal? Will it help you to fulfill your mission? Nothing, no action, is neutral; everything you do either helps you fulfill your mission and accomplish your goals, or moves you further away from them. When you make your decisions based on your personal mission statement, you never regret it.

Now, this doesn't mean that you will never have to do something you don't want to do. On the contrary. There are tasks and obligations that I must fulfill on a regular basis that I don't particularly enjoy, but they get me closer to my ultimate goal, so I do them. Sometimes they are just in line with my values, and so I complete these tasks because they help with the overall picture of who I am or want to become.

To get started with crafting your personal mission statement, take the time to review your answers to the following questions:

1. When you were a child, how did you answer when anyone asked you, "What do you want to be when you grow up?"
2. What special skills or talents do you have?
3. There was a time, it could have been a long time ago, or recently, when you did something that made you feel like you were on top of the world. What was it? What were you doing?
4. What do you like to do? What do you do in your spare time? What do you choose to read about? What are your hobbies?
5. There is something that you do that, when you're doing it, you completely lose track of time. Hours feel like minutes. What is it? What are you doing?
6. What do you have a passion for?
7. How much money do you need/want to make?
8. What does the market need right now?
9. What would you do if you knew you could not fail?

Answering these questions should divulge the purpose within you that's trying to manifest. You'll see a theme developing; you'll feel compelled or driven by a certain idea or set of actions. One thing's for sure, when you've hit on it, you will know it. The thought of accomplishing it will resonate with your core and give you energy you quite possibly never knew you had.

Your mission statement may change slightly over time and that's okay. You may need to modify it based on new levels of awareness and education. Remember that the only constant in life is change. Things change, people change, circumstances change. It's all good. Stephen Covey says, "The key to the ability to change, is a changeless sense of who you are, what you are about, and what you value." Allow yourself the flexibility to grow your mission statement as you grow, refining it as necessary.

Excerpt from the writings of Debra Moorhead, debramoorhead.com

Appendix E

Review of Self-Esteem Research

While much of the research we have culled on self-esteem is from the youth population, much of this knowledge can be generalized to the adult population as well.

Following are excerpts from the booklet Self-Esteem and Youth: What Research Has To Say About It by Robert W. Reasoner. The topics addressed here in brief form are these:

Self-Esteem and Academic Achievement
Alcohol and Drug Abuse
Crime and Violence
Depression and Suicide
Eating Disorders
Interpersonal Relationships
Teenage Pregnancy

SELF-ESTEEM AND ACADEMIC ACHIEVEMENT

There is general agreement that there is a close relationship between self-esteem and academic achievement. However, there is considerable disagreement as to the specific nature of this relationship. It has been argued that students have to do well in school in order to have positive self-esteem or self-concept; another position is that a positive self-esteem is a necessary prerequisite for doing well in school.

Covington(1989) reported that as the level of self-esteem increases, so do achievement scores; as self-esteem decreases, achievement scores decline.

Furthermore, he concluded that self-esteem can be modified through direct instruction and that such instruction can lead to achievement gains.

Specifically, students' perceived efficacy to achieve, combined with personal goal setting, has been found to have a major impact on academic achievement.

Holly (1987) compiled a summary of some 50 studies and indicated that most supported the idea that self-esteem was more likely the result than the cause of academic achievement. He did acknowledge that a certain level of self-esteem is required in order for a student to achieve academic success and that self-esteem and achievement go hand in hand. They feed each other.

Conrath (1986) states that the best way for a child to sustain a sense of confidence is to acquire and demonstrate competence. He found that self-confidence will emerge with success in skill development and learning.

Thus, the key point is to help students set meaningful and realistic goals.

However, the debate about which comes first—a positive self-concept or academic achievement-is more academic than practical. The most important thing is to appreciate the interaction and the reciprocal dynamics between self-concept and achievement. They are mutually reinforcing. While there may be little justification for embarking on a program to raise the level of self-esteem with the intent of raising academic achievement, there are many other justifications for raising self-esteem of students.

It has been my experience that self-esteem programs can be implemented in schools without sacrificing academic excellence and no school has reported a decline in academic achievement while focusing on self-esteem.

ALCOHOL AND DRUG ABUSE

The use of alcohol and drugs among our young people continues to be of serious concern. More than 50% of high school seniors in the U.S. report using illicit drugs and 66% report that they are regular users of alcohol; 71% reported getting drunk and 14% appear to be highly involved with drugs on a regular basis. While a high percentage of youths become involved as a part of the peer social scene, many grow to depend upon drugs or alcohol to fill a personal void.

Studies have found that 18 year olds who used drugs frequently were using them as early as age seven, already more psychologically troubled than their peers. They were already anxious and unhappy, alienated from their family and peers, and overly impulsive. Low self-esteem, lack of conformity, poor academic achievement and poor parental-child relationships are also indicators of young children likely to end up using drugs.

Low self-esteem is the universal common denominator among literally all people suffering from addictions to any and all mind altering substances such as alcohol—not genes. In the book Alcoholism: A False Stigma: Low

Self-Esteem the True Disease, (1996) Candito reports, "Those who have identified themselves as "recovered alcoholics" indicate that low self esteem is the most significant problem in their lives. Low self-esteem is the true problem and the true disease. Alcohol is but a symptom of an alcoholic's disease."

Candito comes to the conclusion that low self-esteem is the underlying origin of all problematic behaviors, and the true disease that plagues the world, resulting in alcohol abuse, drug abuse, and all other obsessive behavior including criminal behavior.

This conclusion is also shared by Andrew Keegan (1987) who maintains that low self-esteem either causes or contributes to neurosis, anxiety, defensiveness, and ultimately alcohol and drug abuse. The reason why some become alcoholic while others do not is dependent upon their ability to contend with low self-esteem.

CRIME AND VIOLENCE

There are multiple factors that contribute to crime and delinquency, making it difficult to determine the role that self-esteem plays. Such factors include drugs, alcohol, hostility, frustration, class and cultural conflict, and jealousy to name but a few.

Johnson(1977) documented that juvenile delinquents not only had low self-esteem, but that they also had higher feelings of anxiety. He concluded that juvenile delinquency prevention programs often fail because they are based on incorrect assumptions about the sources of delinquency and overlook the crucial roles of school failure and low self-esteem.

Kelley(1978) reported a direct correlation between delinquency and low self-esteem. He found evidence of a link between increased self-esteem and a reduction of delinquent behavior. He found that as programs were implemented to raise the level of self-esteem, the incidence of delinquent behavior was reduced.

On the other hand, in a study reported by Ohio State Research News Grabmeier (1988)questions whether low self-esteem does cause delinquency. The study was conducted to test the hypothesis that those with low self-esteem would engage in more delinquent acts to improve their self-esteem. The study found that those with low self-esteem frequently associated with a delinquent support group or gang, but that they did not engage in any more delinquent acts than those with average or above average self-esteem.

Youth join gangs for many reasons, but low self-esteem often is related.

Those with low self-esteem seem to rely more on group or collective self-esteem than those with high personal self-esteem. Thus, some individuals seek gang membership to compensate for feelings of low self-esteem. Sheriff Block of Los Angeles County stated, "Children join gangs to fulfill the need to belong and the need to feel important. They want to be somebody rather than be a nobody. We must focus on enhancing the self-worth and self-esteem of young people so that they do not seek out and need the gang to satisfy these most basic human needs."

Kaplan (1975) conducted extensive studies into the causes of violence, including a study of 7,000 7th graders, and underscores the significance of self-esteem as a factor in crime and violence. He, too, found that violations to self-esteem serve as a major source of hostility and aggression. This conclusion is borne out in the study of those incarcerated for the most violent acts—murder. Gilligan in his study of murderers concludes that low self-esteem is the most common reason for engaging in violence and this is why violent behavior actually increases the self-esteem of those who commit it.

In studies where self-esteem programs have been introduced into the school setting, it has been found that such programs can significantly reduce the incidence of anti-social behavior in schools, as well as reduce vandalism and the incidents of verbal or physical aggression by 40-50%. (Reasoner,1992, Borba, 1999)

DEPRESSION AND SUICIDE

Depression and suicide in young people are major concerns today. Both are closely related to low self-esteem. James Battle (1980) was one of the first to document the close relationship between depression and self-esteem. He discovered several years ago that as depression rises, self-esteem tends to decline, and as self-esteem declines depression rises. However, while low self-esteem correlates closely with depression and suicide, it is neither necessary, nor sufficient, to cause most clinically depressive or suicidal episodes. Often it is the lack of communication skills or close relationships that are necessary for developing and maintaining self-esteem that are the underlying cause.

The difference between a person with high self-esteem and one with low self-esteem isn't how often they get low or even how low they go, but what they do with their low moods. Positive people accept the inevitability of low feelings which will pass, rather than wallowing in their depression.

There is also accumulating evidence that positive self-esteem can be an antidote to depression. Self-esteem serves as a buffer from the onslaught of anxiety, guilt, depression, shame, criticism and other internal attacks.

Since a major source of low self-esteem and depression among adolescents is due to the increased stress currently found among teenagers, helping young people learn how to deal with this anxiety and stress can enable them to work through the stress in an effective way to reduce the impact.

Developing an optimistic outlook on life is also an important quality to develop in children. This means more than just viewing the glass as half-full. It embodies the belief that setbacks are normal and can be overcome by one's own actions. Studies of thousands of children show that those who are pessimistic are much more prone to depression—both in childhood and in adulthood—than those who are optimistic. (Rao, 1994) It is therefore helpful to help children think of more positive thoughts than negative thoughts and to replace negative thoughts with something more positive. This provides a foundation for a positive mental life.

EATING DISORDERS

All the studies done on eating disorders document a strong relationship with self-esteem. Low self-esteem seems to be directly linked with disturbed body image, dropping out of physical activity, eating disorders, substance abuse, abusive relationships and interpersonal problems. Dr. Yellowlees (1996) states that low self-esteem seems to operate as a predisposing and contributory factor in the development of depression, anxiety, eating disorders, alcohol abuse and drug abuse. In some cases, evidence for this relationship is so strong that it is even thought by some researchers that chronic low self-esteem is a necessary prerequisite for disordered eating.

A profile of low self-esteem includes insecurity, negative mood and depression, poor body image, feelings of inadequacy, social and personal withdrawal, poor adaptation skills, and unrealistically high aspirations.

All of these traits are seen fairly consistently in patients with eating disorders.. In addition patients with eating disorders also exhibit other traits associated with low self-esteem.

The teenage years are full of turmoil and changes that can have a detrimental affect on a girl's sense of identity and her self-esteem. Without a strong sense of identity, adolescent girls begin to feel poorly about themselves.

They see the diet as the answer to all their problems. However, they see any failure to stick to their diet as a personal failure. This results in even a lower sense of self-esteem and even more severe dieting. While loss of weight may temporarily boost their self-esteem, it clearly cannot fundamentally alter a deep-seated sense of poor self worth. As a result, self-esteem soon falls, resulting in the individual repeating the dieting process in an attempt to boost self-esteem again. This ultimately leads to greater levels of global dissatisfaction and lower self-esteem.

Women with low self-esteem who are vulnerable to societal pressures for thinness may take on a distorted and negative body image as part of their belief that they can never be worthwhile. An important thing to remember is that most of the underlying psychological factors that lead to an eating disorder are the same for both men and women: low self-esteem, a need to be accepted, depression, anxiety or other existing psychological illness, and an inability to cope with emotions and personal issues.

INTERPERSONAL RELATIONSHIPS

There is a direct relationship between the perception of social success and self-esteem. This success may include confidence in appearance, academic ability, athletic ability, or social relationships. Self-esteem might be viewed then, as a barometer of how well one is doing socially. People seek a certain amount of social acceptance and belonging in order to view themselves as successful and have positive feelings about themselves.

Effective interpersonal relationships are greatly determined by the degree of one's tolerance, open-mindedness and respect for those who are different. To relate most effectively it requires that one not be threatened by the positions of others. A recent series of research studies underscores the importance and role of self-esteem in that process. A series of studies conducted by three professors of psychology at three separate universities acknowledge the infinite variety of cultural perspectives on how mankind views the world. Yet, they found a universal tendency to feel threatened by discrepant viewpoints, combined with a reluctance to change one's own viewpoint.

This seems to be true whether it refers to religion, politics, music, sports, or tastes in wine. Thus, for centuries mankind has tended to respond violently to encounters with different others in defense of their cultural world views.

Through studies conducted by these researchers they found that a critical factor in the type of response one gives is related to one's level of self-esteem. The higher the level of self-esteem, the less individuals feel threatened by different world views. They found that raising the level of self-esteem significantly reduced the level of anxiety and the human response, both emotionally and physiologically. Finally, they concluded that a requirement for cultures that value tolerance, open-mindedness, and respect for those who are different is the fostering of self-esteem.

PREGNANCY AMONG TEENAGE GIRLS

More than one million girls become pregnant every year in the U.S., a rate of teen pregnancy greater than those of other industrialized nations. There is as much research supporting the close relationship between self-esteem and teenage pregnancy as any other problem behavior. Hayes and Fors (1990) report that lower self-esteem is often an antecedent to the engagement in premarital sexual relationships and is more likely to be responsible for teen pregnancies than any other single factor. They found that as self-esteem decreases, sexual attitudes and behavior become more permissive.

Many teenage girls feel that pregnancy is the only alternative to feeling powerless and unimportant. Being pregnant becomes the source of new status, new power and a way to prove to yourself and everyone else that you are capable of being loved and that you have someone who will love you unconditionally. Statistics have shown that 85-90% of the teenage mothers elect to keep their babies rather than give them up for adoption in the belief that a baby will provide the kind of unconditional love and acceptance that they feel they never had.

Studies indicate that a typical profile of teenagers who become pregnant include: being a poor or disinterested student, having low self-esteem, lacking basic skills, looking for someone to love her or something to love, and frequently coming from a dysfunctional family or been sexually abused.

Thus, it is felt that if ways can be found to boost the level of self-esteem of girls, it will be.

From *Self-Esteem and Youth: What Research Has To Say About It*, by Robert W. Reasoner.

Appendix F

Famous quotations on Self-Esteem

I have often found that a good quotation goes a long-way in helping my clients to internalize an idea. You will find that you like some of these quotes more than others. I encourage you to memorize a couple of your favorites and begin incorporating them into your thinking.

Nobody can make you feel inferior without your consent. ~Eleanor Roosevelt

It took me a long time not to judge myself through someone else's eyes. ~Sally Field

We have to learn to be our own best friends because we fall too easily into the trap of being our own worst enemies. ~Roderick Thorp, Rainbow Drive

It ain't what they call you, it's what you answer to. ~W.C. Fields

Whether you think you can or think you can't—you are right. ~Henry Ford

I quit being afraid when my first venture failed and the sky didn't fall down. ~Allen H. Neuharth

If you hear a voice within you say "you cannot paint," then by all means paint, and that voice will be silenced. ~Vincent Van Gogh

Make the most of yourself, for that is all there is of you. ~Ralph Waldo Emerson

I am convinced all of humanity is born with more gifts than we know. Most are born geniuses and just get de-geniused rapidly. ~Buckminster Fuller

Let me never fall into the vulgar mistake of dreaming that I am persecuted whenever I am contradicted. ~Ralph Waldo Emerson

People are like stained-glass windows. They sparkle and shine when the sun is out, but when the darkness sets in their true beauty is revealed only if there is light from within. ~Elisabeth Kübler-Ross

Don't live down to expectations. Go out there and do something remarkable. ~Wendy Wasserstein

Success comes in cans, not cant's. ~Author Unknown

Put your future in good hands—your own. ~Author Unknown

I am not a has-been. I am a will be. ~Lauren Bacall

The light of starry dreams can only be seen once we escape the blinding cities of disbelief. ~Shawn Purvis, ShawnPurvis.com

If you really put a small value upon yourself, rest assured that the world will not raise your price. ~Author Unknown

Confidence comes not from always being right but from not fearing to be wrong. ~Peter T. Mcintyre

Life shrinks or expands in proportion to one's courage. ~Anaïs Nin, Diary, 1969

Argue for your limitations and, sure enough, they're yours. ~Richard Bach, Illusions

You have to expect things of yourself before you can do them. ~Michael Jordan

It is not the mountain we conquer but ourselves. ~Edmund Hillary

Thousands of geniuses live and die undiscovered—either by themselves or by others. ~Mark Twain

Aerodynamically the bumblebee shouldn't be able to fly, but the bumblebee doesn't know that so it goes on flying anyway. ~Mary Kay Ash

Without a humble but reasonable confidence in your own powers you cannot be successful or happy. ~Norman Vincent Peale

The courage to be is the courage to accept oneself, in spite of being unacceptable. ~Paul Tillich

Of all our infirmities, the most savage is to despise our being. ~Michel de Montaigne

People are crying up the rich and variegated plumage of the peacock, and he is himself blushing at the sight of his ugly feet. ~Sa'Di

It's hard to fight an enemy who has outposts in your head. ~Sally Kempton, Esquire, 1970

When the grass looks greener on the other side of the fence, it may be that they take better care of it there. ~Cecil Selig

Other people's opinion of you does not have to become your reality. ~Les Brown

You have brains in your head.
You have feet in your shoes.
You can steer yourself in any direction you choose.
You're on your own.
And you know what you know.
You are the guy who'll decide where to go.
~Dr. Seuss

Confidence is preparation. Everything else is beyond your control. ~Richard Kline

I have great faith in fools; self-confidence my friends call it. ~Edgar Allan Poe

What lies behind us and what lies before us are tiny matters compared to what lies within us. ~Henry S. Haskins, Meditations in Wall Street, 1940, commonly misattributed to Ralph Waldo Emerson (Thanks, Garson O'Toole!)

Never dull your shine for somebody else. ~Tyra Banks, America's Next Top Model, "The Girl Who Is Afraid of Heights," original airdate 17 October 2007

If we all did the things we are capable of doing, we would literally astound ourselves. ~Thomas Alva Edison

Always hold your head up, but be careful to keep your nose at a friendly level. ~Max L. Forman

Our doubts are traitors, and make us lose the good we oft might win, by fearing to attempt. ~William Shakespeare, Measure for Measure, 1604

Just as much as we see in others we have in ourselves. ~William Hazlitt

Your problem is you're . . . too busy holding onto your unworthiness. ~Ram Dass

Learning too soon our limitations, we never learn our powers. ~Mignon McLaughlin, The Neurotic's Notebook, 1960

Lend yourself to others, but give yourself to yourself. ~Michel de Montaigne

It's me who is my enemy
Me who beats me up
Me who makes the monsters
Me who strips my confidence.
~Paula Cole, "Me," This Fire

The man who acquires the ability to take full possession of his own mind may take possession of anything else to which he is justly entitled. -Andrew Carnegie

Life marks us all down, so it's just as well that we start out by overpricing ourselves. -Mignon McLaughlin, The Neurotic's Notebook, 1960

A gold medal is a nice thing—but if you're not enough without it, you'll never be enough with it. -From Cool Runnings

I've spent most of my life walking under that hovering cloud, jealousy, whose acid raindrops blurred my vision and burned holes in my heart. Once I learned to use the umbrella of confidence, the skies cleared up for me and the sunshine called joy became my faithful companion. -Astrid Alauda

Don't let anyone steal your dream. It's your dream, not theirs. -Dan Zadra

If I am not for myself, who will be? -Pirkei Avot

All of us have wonders hidden in our breasts, only needing circumstances to evoke them. -Charles Dickens

Once you become self-conscious, there is no end to it; once you start to doubt, there is no room for anything else. -Mignon McLaughlin, The Neurotic's Notebook, 1960

What a man thinks of himself, that it is which determines, or rather indicates his fate. -Henry David Thoreau

A person can grow only as much as his horizon allows. ~John Powell

Plant your own garden and decorate your own soul, instead of waiting for someone to bring you flowers. ~Veronica A. Shoffstall, "After a While," 1971

If you must love your neighbor as yourself, it is at least as fair to love yourself as your neighbor. ~Nicholas de Chamfort

I am not afraid of storms for I am learning how to sail my ship. ~Louisa May Alcott

How often in life we complete a task that was beyond the capability of the person we were when we started it. ~Robert Brault, www.robertbrault.com

Every day we slaughter our finest impulses. That is why we get a heart-ache when we read those lines written by the hand of a master and recognize them as our own, as the tender shoots which we stifled because we lacked the faith to believe in our own powers, our own criterion of truth and beauty. Every man, when he gets quiet, when he becomes desperately honest with himself, is capable of uttering profound truths. We all derive from the same source. There is no mystery about the origin of things. We are all part of creation, all kings, all poets, all musicians; we have only to open up, to discover what is already there. ~Henry Miller, Sexus

Pay no attention to what the critics say. A statue has never been erected in honor of a critic. ~Jean Sibelius

Self-confidence grows on trees, in other people's orchards. ~Mignon McLaughlin, The Neurotic's Notebook, 1960

When there is no enemy within, the enemies outside cannot hurt you. ~African Proverb

The best way to gain self-confidence is to do what you are afraid to do. ~Author Unknown

Be proud to wear you. ~Dodinsky, www.dodinsky.com

Be humble, for the worst thing in the world is of the same stuff as you; be confident, for the stars are of the same stuff as you. ~Nicholai Velimirovic

Great tranquility of heart is his who cares for neither praise nor blame. ~Thomas à Kempis

Shyness has a strange element of narcissism, a belief that how we look, how we perform, is truly important to other people. ~André Dubus

Chiefly the mold of a man's fortune is in his own hands. ~Francis Bacon

God wisely designed the human body so that we can neither pat our own backs nor kick ourselves too easily. ~Author Unknown

We probably wouldn't worry about what people think of us if we could know how seldom they do. ~Olin Miller

As soon

Seek roses in December, ice in June;
Hope constancy in wind, or corn in chaff;
Believe a woman or an epitaph,
Or any other thing that's false, before
You trust in critics.
~George Gordon, Lord Byron, "English Bards and Scotch Reviewers"

You're never as good as everyone tells you when you win, and you're never as bad as they say when you lose. ~Lou Holtz and John Heisler, The Fighting Spirit

All that Adam had, all that Caesar could, you have and can do . . . . Build, therefore, your own world. ~Ralph Waldo Emerson, Nature

Oliver Wendell Holmes once attended a meeting in which he was the shortest man present. "Dr. Holmes," quipped a friend, "I should think you'd feel rather small among us big fellows." "I do," retorted Holmes, "I feel like a dime among a lot of pennies." ~Author Unknown

The way you treat yourself sets the standard for others. ~Sonya Friedman

Our ordinary mind always tries to persuade us that we are nothing but acorns and that our greatest happiness will be to become bigger, fatter, shinier acorns; but that is of interest only to pigs. Our faith gives us knowledge of something better: that we can become oak trees. ~E.F. Schumacher

Only as high as I reach can I grow,
Only as far as I seek can I go,
Only as deep as I look can I see,

Only as much as I dream can I be.
~Karen Ravn

Our deepest fear is not that we are inadequate. Our deepest fear is that we are powerful beyond measure. It is our light, not our darkness that most frightens us. We ask ourselves, Who am I to be brilliant, gorgeous, talented, fabulous? Actually, who are you not to be? You are a child of God. Your playing small does not serve the world. There is nothing enlightened about shrinking so that other people won't feel insecure around you. We are all meant to shine, as children do. We were born to make manifest the glory of God that is within us. It is not just in some of us; it is in everyone. And as we let our own light shine, we unconsciously give other people permission to do the same. As we are liberated from our own fear, our presence automatically liberates others. ~Marianne Williamson, A Return to Love: Reflections on the Principles of "A Course in Miracles," 1992 (commonly misattributed to Nelson Mandela, 1994 inauguration speech)

Men are not against you; they are merely for themselves. ~Gene Fowler, Skyline, 1961

No power in society, no hardship in your condition can depress you, keep you down, in knowledge, power, virtue, influence, but by your own consent. ~William Ellery Channing, 1838 (Thanks, Garson O'Toole!)

All quotes from Quotegarden.com

Made in the USA
Lexington, KY
19 October 2014